PIANO · VOCAL · GUITAR

NICOLE C. MULLEN
THE ULTIMATE COLLECTION

ISBN 978-1-4234-7713-6

HAL · LEONARD®
CORPORATION

7777 W. BLUEMOUND RD. P.O. BOX 13819 MILWAUKEE, WI 53213

Visit Hal Leonard Online at
www.halleonard.com

ALWAYS LOVE YOU

Words and Music by
NICOLE C. MULLEN

Moderate Pop Ballad

Tell me, ___ if you break the ho-ur-glass, ___ can you
miss you ___ and the fun-ny things ___ you ___ say. ___ I re-

hold to what ___ you have? ___ Can you make the mo-ment last? ___
mem-ber ev-'ry day ___ in a hun-dred dif-f'rent ways. ___ I

Tell me, ___ if you give a-way ___ your heart, ___ and the
miss you ___ be-ing here ___ with me. ___

COME UNTO ME

Words and Music by
NICOLE C. MULLEN

BLACK, WHITE, TAN

Words and Music by NICOLE C. MULLEN
and DAVID MULLEN

Ma-ma looks like cof-fee, Dad-dy looks like cream. ___ Ba-by is a mo-cha drop A-
Ev-'ry-one is pre-cious in the Fa-ther's sight. ___ It don't mat-ter, red or yel-low,
Na ___ na na na na na na na na na. ___ Na na na na na na na na

mer-i-can dream. ___ All the col-ors of the rain-bow ___ are in her
black or ___ white. ___ He just loves you 'cause He loves you; ___ I tell you,
na na ___ na. ___ Na na na na na na na na, ___

fam-'ly tree, ___ wo-ven all to-geth-er in a
this is true. ___ You are not a col-or and a
na na na. ___ Na na na na na na na na

CALL ON JESUS

Words and Music by
NICOLE C. MULLEN

CONVINCED

Words and Music by NICOLE C. MULLEN,
DAVID HENTSCHEL and NICK MOROCH

Moderately

I don't know ___ if light is bright-er in the earth ___ or the soul. ___ And I don't know ___ which night is dark-er: the one I do ___ or don't know. ___ But I'm con-vinced, ___

* Recorded a half step lower.

EVERYDAY PEOPLE

Words and Music by
SYLVESTER STEWART

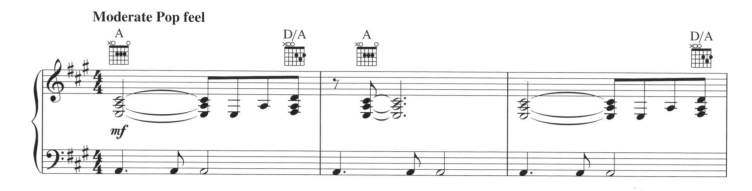

Some - times I'm right, and I can be wrong. __
I'm no bet - ter and nei - ther are you. __

My own be - liefs __ are in my songs. __ The butch - er, the bank - er, the
We're all the same, __ what - ev - er you do. __ You love me, you hate me, you

FAITH, HOPE & LOVE

Words and Music by
MARK SCHULTZ

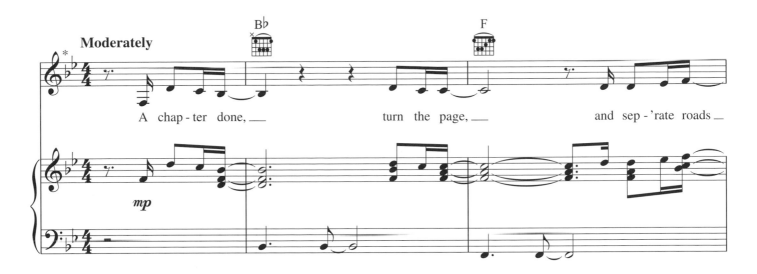

A chap-ter done, __ turn the page, __ and sep-'rate roads __

__ lead sep-'rate ways. __ But as we go, __ we're not __ a - lone, __

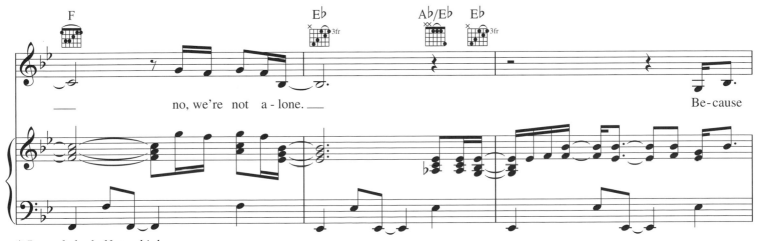

__ no, we're not a - lone. __ Be-cause

* *Recorded a half step higher.*

FOLLOW JESUS
(Landa Yesu)

Words and Music by TONY WOOD,
CHAD CATES, TODD SMITH
and JAMES SMITH

* Recorded a half step lower.

yeah, ___ yeah.   Let Your truth ___ be ___ told, ___

let our hearts ___ re - ceive. ___   May we all ___ be ___ changed. ___

To Coda   Let us now ___ be - lieve. ___   Fol - low Je -

- sus. _____   Nge ta vu - lu -

Ban - dun - du ban - tu ya Bi - ble.   Ban - dun - du ban - tu ya Bi - ble.

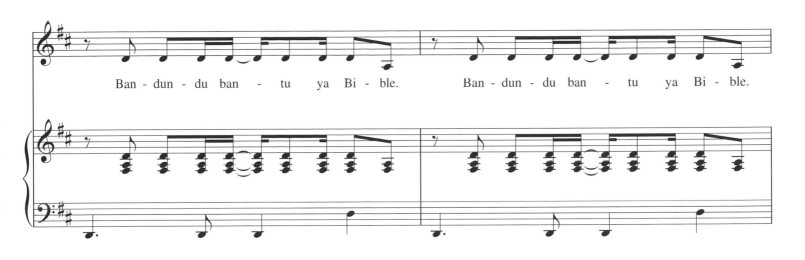

Ban - dun - du ban - tu ya Bible. Ban - dun - du ban - tu ya Bi - ble.

Ban - dun - du ban - tu ya Bible. Ban - dun - du ban - tu ya Bi - ble.

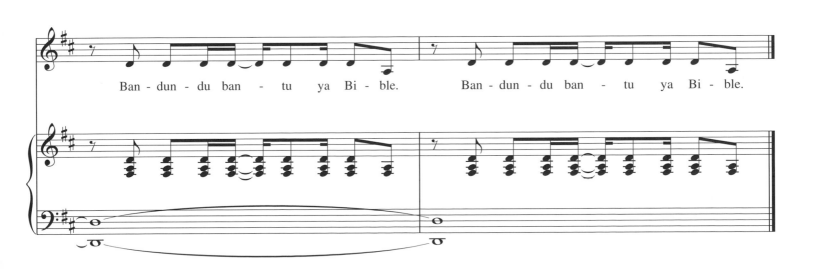

Ban - dun - du ban - tu ya Bible. Ban - dun - du ban - tu ya Bi - ble.

FOREVER YOU REIGN

Words and Music by
NICOLE C. MULLEN

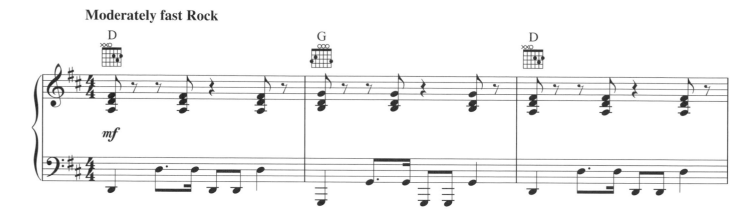

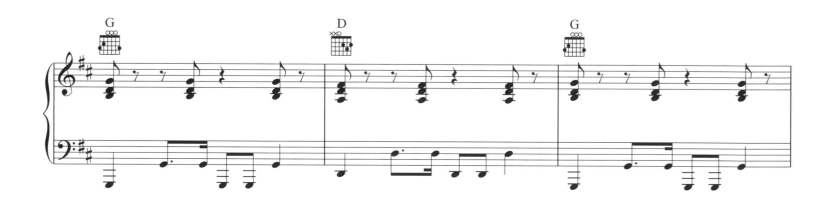

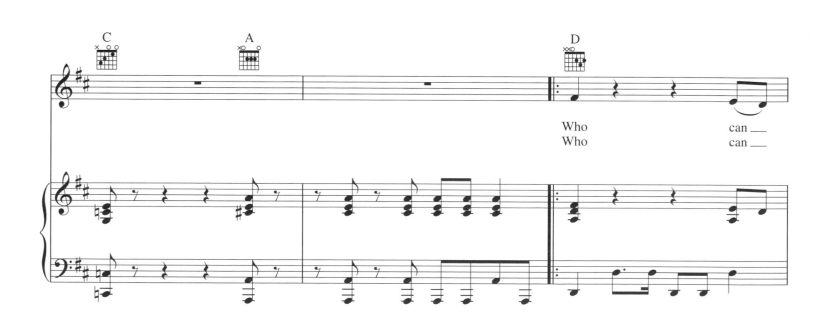

Who   can ___
Who   can ___

FREEDOM

Words and Music by
NICOLE C. MULLEN

Syncopated dance beat

I AM

Words and Music by NICOLE C. MULLEN
and DAVID MULLEN

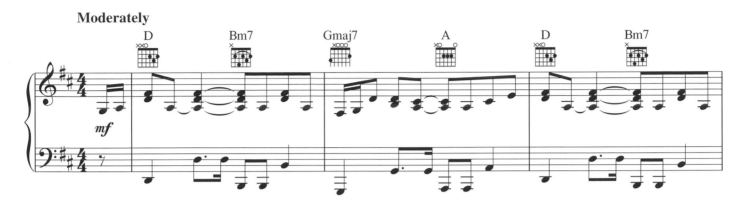

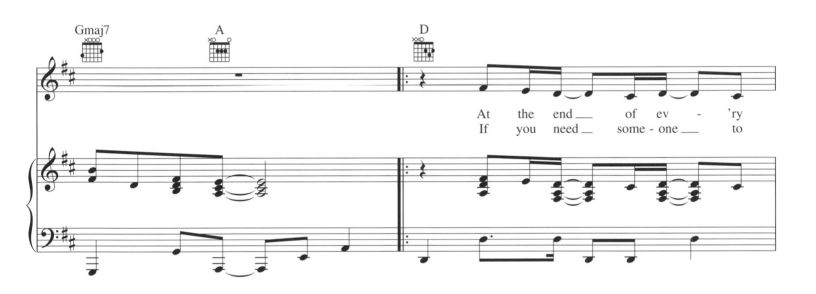

At the end ___ of ev - 'ry
If you need ___ some - one ___ to

rain - bow ___   there's a prom - ise prov - en
hold ___ you ___ 'cause your world's ___ fall - ing a -

I WISH

Words and Music by
NICOLE C. MULLEN

Gentle Ballad

wish I ____ could ____ paint your world ____ so beau - ti - ful, ____ and I

strength. Your heart __ and __ soul, your mind __ and

strength. Your heart __ and __ soul, your mind and

strength.

LAMB OF GOD

Words and Music by NICOLE C. MULLEN
and DAVID MULLEN

Freely

Moderately slow groove

Once up-on a long night, af-ter a hard ride, some-
wise men? A star did guide them,

where in Beth-le-hem,___ a ba-by breaks the si-lence. Sweet-ly He's cry-ing,____ "I
search-ing all___ the earth___ 'til they found the one Child, the ver-y God-Child___ who

am Em-man-u-el."___ Then an-gels gave Him mu-sic, shep-herds gave rev-'rence and a
ruled the u-ni-verse.___ Did they know the la-dy's lit-tle ba-by was

ON MY KNEES

Words and Music by NICOLE C. MULLEN,
DAVID MULLEN and MICHAEL OCHS

MUSIC OF MY HEART

Words and Music by
NICOLE C. MULLEN

I'm not a-shamed to tell the whole world, oh, with-out You I'm noth-ing at all, that I have strings in need of mend-ing,

the song that holds me in the dark,

the fire that warms me when I'm cold,

the sym - pho - ny that calms my

fear, the lyr - ic that I long to hear,

ONE TOUCH
(Press)

Words and Music by
NICOLE C. MULLEN

* Recorded a half step lower.

REDEEMER

Words and Music by
NICOLE C. MULLEN

The ver - y same deem - er, _____ He lives to take a - way my shame. _____ And He _____ lives; for - ev - er I'll pro - claim _____ that the

SHOOBY

Words and Music by
NICOLE C. MULLEN

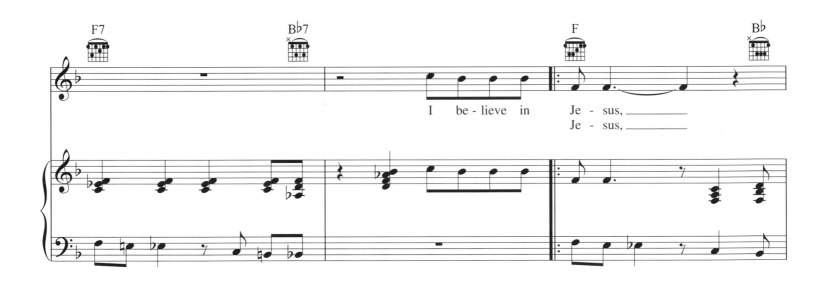

I be - lieve in Je - sus, _____
Je - sus, _____

and I won't a - pol - o - gize. _____
I'm a fa - nat - ic bo - na fide. _____

He has bought __ me my
When I think a - bout His

TALK ABOUT IT

Words and Music by NICOLE C. MULLEN
and BROOKE DOZIER

Recorded a half step lower.

To Coda ⊕

Let the re-deemed of the Lord say so. Talk a-bout it, say so.

Talk, talk a-bout it. From Bang - la - desh to Ban - gor, Maine,

if you're talk - in' 'bout His name, give Him glo - ry un - a - shamed.

His love is so ex - cit - ing. Say it loud or qui - et - ly,

STILL A DREAM

Words and Music by NICOLE C. MULLEN,
DAVID MULLEN and GERRY STOBER

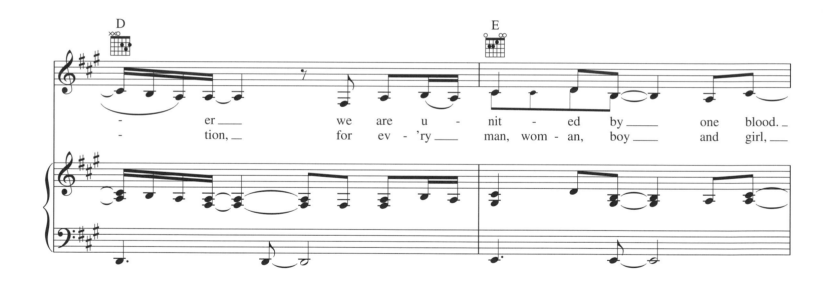